What Holiday is Today?

A Brief History of Holidays in The U.S.A.

T.A. Romero

Table of Contents

Veterans Day - Honoring Service, Sacrifice, and Patriotism (November 11th)

Thanksgiving Day - A Time for Gratitude and Unity (Fourth Thursday in November)

Christmas Day - Celebrating the Joy of the Season (December 25th)

Part 2: Regional and Cultural Holidays
Mardi Gras - Revelry, Tradition, and Cultural Extravaganza (typically falls in February)

St. Patrick's Day - Irish Heritage and Festive Merriment (March 17th)

Diwali - The Festival of Lights and Cultural Celebration (between mid-October to mid-November)

Hanukkah - The Festival of Lights and Jewish Heritage (varies each year based on the Hebrew calendar)

Eid al-Fitr - Celebrating the Festival of Breaking the Fast (varies each year based on the Islamic lunar calendar)

Chinese New Year - Embracing Tradition and Renewal (falls between late January and mid-February)

Cinco de Mayo - Celebrating Mexican Heritage and Unity (May 5th)

Oktoberfest - A Bavarian Celebration in the United States (typically takes place in September or October)

Conclusion

Introduction

Welcome to this exciting journey through the vibrant tapestry of holidays celebrated in the United States. Within the pages of this book, we invite you to embark on an exploration of the cultural, historical, and social significance of these cherished occasions that punctuate our lives and bring communities together.

Holidays are the threads that weave the fabric of our collective memory, connecting us to the past, grounding us in the present, and inspiring us for the future. They are the markers of time, the anchors of tradition, and the gateways to cherished memories. Through rituals, customs, and celebrations, they provide us with moments of respite from the routine of daily life and allow us to reconnect with our roots, our values, and our shared humanity.

In this book, we have sought to unravel the stories behind each holiday, delving into their origins, their evolution, and their significance in the American cultural landscape. As we turn the pages, we will traverse a diverse tapestry of celebrations that reflect the mosaic of cultures, beliefs, and experiences that make up the United States.

From the solemn remembrance of Memorial Day to the joyous revelry of Mardi Gras, from the reflections of Thanksgiving to the exuberance of Independence Day fireworks, each holiday has its own unique tale to tell. We will uncover the historical events, the cultural traditions, and the collective memories that have shaped these occasions into what they are today.

Throughout this journey, we will encounter the stories of remarkable individuals whose legacies have become inseparable from the holidays we celebrate. From civil rights leaders like Martin Luther King Jr. to visionary presidents like Abraham Lincoln, their contributions have left an indelible mark on the tapestry of American holidays. We will explore the movements they sparked, the ideals they championed, and the enduring impact they have had on our collective consciousness.

But this is not just a book about history; it is a celebration of the present and an invitation to embrace the diversity that defines our nation. We will immerse ourselves in the vibrant colors, flavors, and sounds that fill the air during cultural festivals like Diwali, Chinese New Year, and Eid al-Fitr. We will explore the traditions, the music, the dance, and the culinary delights that bring communities together in joyous unity.

In each chapter, we will endeavor to capture the essence of the holiday, to convey the emotions, the atmosphere, and the spirit that infuses these cherished moments. We will strive to paint vivid pictures with words, to transport you to the bustling streets of New Orleans during Mardi Gras, to the solemn rows of gravestones on a Memorial Day commemoration, to the family gatherings around a Thanksgiving table laden with abundance.

As you journey through this book, we encourage you to pause, to reflect, and to engage with the stories that unfold. Each holiday is an opportunity to deepen our understanding of the world around us, to appreciate the tapestry of cultures that have shaped our nation, and to forge connections with our fellow human beings.

We hope that this book will serve as a source of inspiration, enlightenment, and celebration and encourage you to embrace the spirit of these holidays, to honor their traditions, and to find joy in the rituals that mark our shared existence.

Above all, may it remind us that, despite our differences, we are united by the universal desire to come together, to celebrate, and to find meaning in the milestones of life. Holidays are the threads that bind us, the moments that remind us of our common humanity, and the tapestry that weaves our collective story.

So, we invite you to turn the page and embark on this journey with us. Let us uncover the beauty, the diversity, and the timeless traditions that make up the tapestry of holidays in the United States. Together, let us celebrate, remember, and embrace the rich tapestry of our shared human experience.

Part 1: Federal Holidays

New Year's Day - A Tapestry of Time: The Evolution of New Year's Day in the United States

(January 1st)

New Year's Day in the United States holds a special place in the hearts of Americans as a holiday symbolizing new beginnings, fresh opportunities, and the chance to reflect on the past year. The history of New Year's Day in the United States is a fascinating journey that weaves together ancient traditions, cultural influences, and historical events that have shaped its celebration over time. In this chapter, we delve into the rich tapestry of New Year's Day, exploring its origins, cultural significance, and the evolution of its observance in the United States.

Ancient Origins
To truly understand the history of New Year's Day, we must first explore its ancient origins. We embark on a journey back in time to the civilizations of Babylon and Rome, where the foundation for New Year's celebrations was laid. In Babylon, we witness the grand festival of Akitu, a joyous event where people gather to honor their gods, seek blessings for the year ahead, and participate in colorful processions and ceremonies. The festival's influence on the concept of New Year's Day echoes through the ages. Similarly, in ancient Rome, we delve into the festive atmosphere of Saturnalia, a celebration filled with feasting, gift exchanges, and revelry that marked the turning of the year.

Colonial Beginnings
As European settlers arrived in the American colonies, they brought with them their own New Year's customs and traditions. In this section, we explore how early celebrations in colonial America were influenced by religious observances and community gatherings. We delve into the diverse practices of different regions and cultural groups, highlighting

the ways in which these customs shaped the early observance of New Year's Day. From the Dutch settlers' New Year's Eve parties in New Amsterdam (now New York City) to the Scottish practice of "first-footing," we uncover the cultural tapestry that characterized the colonial celebrations.

Changing Times: From Religious Observances to Personal Reflection

The 19th century witnessed a shift in the celebration of New Year's Day in the United States. In this section, we delve into the changing attitudes towards the holiday, as it transformed from predominantly religious observances to a day of personal reflection and self-improvement. We explore the rise of New Year's resolutions, the practice of setting goals for the coming year, and the increasing emphasis on self-improvement. Drawing on historical accounts, personal narratives, and cultural references, we paint a vivid picture of how Americans embraced the concept of personal growth and renewal on New Year's Day.

The Influence of Immigrant Traditions

One cannot discuss the history of New Year's Day in the United States without acknowledging the influence of immigrant traditions. In this section, we dive into the diverse cultural influences that have shaped the American celebration of New Year's Day. From the German tradition of "Silvester" and the Irish "Hogmanay" to the Hispanic observances of "Nochevieja," we explore how these immigrant customs became woven into the fabric of American celebrations, enriching the tapestry of New Year's Day.

Establishment as a Federal Holiday

In 1870, the formal recognition of January 1st as a federal holiday in the United States was a result of significant debates, legislative efforts, cultural shifts, and the involvement of key figures and events. It was a pivotal moment in the history of New Year's Day. The debates surrounding the establishment of this national holiday revolved around questions of tradition, cultural identity, and the need for a unifying celebration that would resonate with all Americans. Legislative efforts were undertaken to formalize the holiday's status and ensure its observance across the nation. These efforts required the passage of legislation and the coordination of government agencies and institutions. Cultural shifts played a crucial role in shaping public perception and support for recognizing January 1st as a federal holiday. Society's evolving values, ideals, and aspirations influenced the demand for a national day of reflection, unity, and hope. Key figures emerged during this period, advocating for the recognition of New Year's Day. They championed the importance of celebrating this day as a symbol of national unity and a time for personal introspection and renewal. Events, such as public gatherings, rallies, and cultural festivals, also played a significant role in raising awareness and garnering support for the establishment of the holiday. These events provided platforms for communities to come together, share their traditions, and showcase the cultural diversity that enriches the fabric of American society. The culmination of these debates, legislative efforts, cultural shifts, key figures, and events resulted in the official recognition of New Year's Day as a federal holiday in 1870, solidifying its place in the national calendar and affirming its importance as a day of collective celebration and reflection.

Modern-Day Celebrations and Traditions

The final section of this chapter immerses us in the modern-day celebrations and traditions of New Year's Day in the United States. We are transported to bustling city streets adorned with vibrant lights, where the atmosphere crackles with anticipation. The night sky comes alive with a spectacular display of fireworks, illuminating the darkness and evoking a sense of awe and wonder. People of all ages gather in public squares, their faces illuminated by the warm glow of the festivities. Laughter and joy fill the air as families and friends come together, sharing hugs, exchanging well wishes, and toasting to the promise of a new year. Resilient spirits are uplifted, and hearts are filled with a renewed sense of hope and optimism. Amidst the laughter and merriment, individuals take quiet moments to reflect on the past year, contemplating their achievements, and setting aspirations for the future. New Year's resolutions are made with earnest determination, a collective commitment to personal growth and self-improvement. It is a time of cherished traditions, from the clinking of champagne glasses to the singing of "Auld Lang Syne," a bittersweet melody that evokes memories of times gone by. The celebration of New Year's Day in the United States is a symphony of sights, sounds, and emotions, capturing the essence of unity, renewal, and the boundless possibilities that lie ahead.

In this captivating chapter, we have delved deep into the history of New Year's Day in the United States. From its ancient origins to its evolution in the American colonies, the shifting cultural influences, and the establishment of the holiday as a national observance, we have explored the multifaceted tapestry of this beloved holiday. As we conclude this chapter, we reflect on the timeless significance of New Year's Day, a day that continues to inspire hope, reflection, and the pursuit of personal growth.

The History of Martin Luther King Jr. Day - A Triumph of Equality and Justice

(Third Monday in January)

The Seeds of Recognition

In the aftermath of Dr. Martin Luther King Jr.'s assassination on April 4, 1968, the nation was gripped by grief and a renewed sense of urgency to honor his memory. Grassroots movements and civil rights organizations began advocating for a dedicated day to commemorate Dr. King's life and work. The resonance of his teachings, such as the iconic "I Have a Dream" speech, served as a powerful catalyst for the growing desire to recognize his contributions to the struggle for racial equality.

The Legislative Battle

The path to establishing Martin Luther King Jr. Day as a national holiday was marked by a challenging legislative battle. Activists, lawmakers, and supporters faced resistance and opposition in their efforts to secure official recognition. Coretta Scott King, Dr. King's widow, played a significant role in rallying public support and testifying before Congress to emphasize the importance of honoring her husband's work. Numerous bills and proposals were introduced, triggering debates and discussions that propelled the cause forward.

A National Observance

The culmination of the legislative battle came on November 2, 1983, when President Ronald Reagan signed the Martin Luther King Jr. Day Bill into law, designating the third Monday in January as a federal holiday to honor Dr. King. This momentous event not only recognized Dr. King's contributions to American society but also symbolized the nation's commitment to equality, justice, and the ongoing fight against racism. The signing of the bill marked a significant turning point in American history.

State Adoption and Cultural Significance

Following the federal recognition, each state gradually adopted Martin Luther King Jr. Day as a holiday, albeit at different times and with varying approaches. State-level adoption allowed for diverse celebrations and observances, including marches, rallies, educational programs, and artistic expressions. These activities became an integral part of the holiday's cultural significance, fostering dialogue, promoting understanding, and highlighting the ongoing struggle for racial equality.

Reflection and Transformation

Martin Luther King Jr. Day serves as a powerful catalyst for reflection and transformation. It prompts individuals and communities to examine the enduring relevance of Dr. King's teachings in contemporary society. The holiday inspires people to take action against injustice, working towards a more equitable and inclusive future. Through acts of service, educational initiatives, and the amplification of Dr. King's messages, individuals contribute to the ongoing fight for equality and justice, fulfilling the vision that Dr. King championed throughout his life.

The history of Martin Luther King Jr. Day is a testament to the power of perseverance, activism, and the collective commitment to justice and equality. From the seeds of recognition to the legislative battles, the nationwide observance of the holiday symbolizes the enduring legacy of Dr. King and the indomitable spirit of those who fought for civil rights. Martin Luther King Jr. Day serves as a reminder of the ongoing struggle for racial equality and social justice, inspiring individuals to continue the work of creating a more inclusive and equitable society.

Presidents' Day - Honoring the Leaders of a Nation

(Third Monday in February)

Origins and Early Celebrations

Presidents' Day has its origins in the desire to pay tribute to George Washington, the first president of the United States. Early celebrations of Washington's birthday began to emerge in the late 18th century, shortly after his retirement from public service. Friends and associates of Washington organized private gatherings to honor his contributions and express their gratitude for his leadership during the formative years of the nation. These intimate commemorations served as a testament to the deep respect and admiration held for Washington by those who knew him personally.

Expanding to Honor All U.S. Presidents

As the United States continued to grow and evolve, the scope of Presidents' Day expanded to encompass the legacies of all U.S. presidents. The recognition of Washington's unparalleled leadership paved the way for acknowledging the contributions of other presidents who had left indelible marks on the nation's history. Abraham Lincoln, with his unwavering commitment to preserving the Union and emancipating the enslaved, became an iconic figure in the expanded celebration of Presidents' Day. The inclusion of other transformative presidents, such as Thomas Jefferson, Franklin D. Roosevelt, and many more, further enriched the holiday's significance.

The Pursuit of a National Holiday

The establishment of Presidents' Day as a national holiday required a concerted effort to secure widespread recognition. Various initiatives were undertaken to promote the importance of honoring the nation's presidents. Lawmakers, activists, and citizens alike championed the cause, emphasizing the significance of celebrating the presidency as a symbol of American democracy and leadership. Through petitions, public discourse, and the tireless advocacy of passionate individuals, Presidents' Day gradually gained momentum and became a subject of legislative consideration.

Traditions and Celebrations

Presidents' Day is synonymous with a range of traditions and celebrations that capture the spirit of the holiday. Across the United States, communities come together to honor the presidency through diverse activities and events. Grand parades grace the streets, featuring floats adorned with images of iconic presidents and marching bands playing patriotic tunes. Historical reenactments transport audiences back to significant moments in presidential history, offering a glimpse into the challenges and triumphs of past administrations. Educational programs and exhibits showcase the achievements and impact of various presidents, inviting citizens to deepen their understanding of the nation's leadership.

Reflection and National Identity

Presidents' Day provides a meaningful opportunity for reflection on the nation's history, values, and the role of its presidents in shaping its identity. It prompts individuals to contemplate the qualities that define effective leadership and the challenges faced by presidents throughout history. Citizens engage in conversations about the nation's progress, its democratic institutions, and the responsibilities of an engaged citizenry. Presidents' Day becomes a time of introspection, fostering a sense of national identity and inspiring individuals to contribute actively to the betterment of their communities and the country as a whole.

Presidents' Day stands as a testament to the enduring legacy of American leadership, as well as the collective achievements and challenges faced by the nation's presidents. From its humble beginnings as a celebration of George Washington's birthday, the holiday has expanded to encompass all U.S. presidents, offering a profound opportunity for reflection, celebration, and national unity. As Americans gather to commemorate Presidents' Day, they honor the leadership that has shaped the nation's history, embrace the principles of democracy, and aspire to build a brighter future for all.

Memorial Day - Honoring the Sacrifice of America's Heroes

(Last Monday in May)

Memorial Day holds a sacred place in the hearts of Americans, serving as a solemn reminder of the men and women who have made the ultimate sacrifice while serving in the U.S. military. In this chapter, we embark on a poignant journey through the history, traditions, and significance of Memorial Day. From its origins as Decoration Day to its evolution into a national holiday of remembrance, we explore the profound impact of this solemn occasion on the collective memory and gratitude of a nation.

Origins and Evolution:
Memorial Day finds its roots in the aftermath of the American Civil War, a conflict that claimed the lives of countless soldiers and left scars on the nation's soul. In the wake of this devastation, communities across the country began organizing gatherings to decorate the graves of fallen soldiers with flowers and flags. These local observances sought to provide solace to grieving families and pay homage to the bravery and sacrifice of those who gave their lives for their country. As these commemorative events gained prominence, the concept of Decoration Day emerged.

The Birth of Decoration Day:

Decoration Day, as it was initially known, saw its first official commemoration on May 30, 1868. General John A. Logan, the commander-in-chief of the Grand Army of the Republic, proclaimed this date as a time for the nation to come together and honor the fallen soldiers by decorating their graves. The date of May 30 was chosen intentionally as it did not coincide with any specific battle anniversary, allowing for a universal recognition of sacrifice. Communities across the United States embraced the call to decorate the graves of fallen soldiers, further solidifying the significance of Decoration Day.

Transformation into Memorial Day:
In the years following its establishment, Decoration Day evolved both in name and purpose. The term "Memorial Day" gradually replaced "Decoration Day" in popular usage, reflecting a broader focus on memorializing all fallen soldiers, regardless of the conflict in which they served. The end of World War I brought about a significant shift in the nation's perception of Memorial Day, as it became a day to honor the sacrifices of soldiers from all wars. In 1971, Memorial Day was officially designated as a national holiday, observed on the last Monday in May.

Traditions and Observances:
Memorial Day is a day of solemn remembrance, and its observance varies throughout the United States. Communities engage in various traditions and ceremonies that pay tribute to fallen heroes. Many people visit cemeteries to decorate graves with flowers, flags, and other symbols of remembrance. Memorial services and parades take place, providing a platform for community members to express their gratitude and reflect on the sacrifices made by the brave men and women in uniform. In recent years, initiatives like the "National Moment of Remembrance" have emerged to encourage a moment of unity and reflection at 3:00 p.m. local time on Memorial Day.

National Symbols of Remembrance:
Symbols play an essential role in honoring the fallen on Memorial Day. The American flag, with its stars and stripes, holds a prominent position in commemorative ceremonies. Flag etiquette is observed, with flags raised to full staff and then lowered to half-staff until noon as a mark of respect for the fallen. The "National Moment of Remembrance" is often signaled by a bugler playing "Taps," a hauntingly beautiful melody that evokes a sense of reverence and reflection.

Remembering and Honoring the Fallen:
Above all, Memorial Day serves as a poignant reminder to cherish the freedoms and liberties that the fallen soldiers fought to protect. It is a day to express gratitude for the selflessness and bravery of those who made the ultimate sacrifice. Americans

participate in acts of remembrance, from visiting memorials and military monuments to engaging in charitable acts that support the families of fallen soldiers. It is through these gestures of gratitude and remembrance that the spirit of Memorial Day lives on, ensuring that the sacrifices of America's heroes are never forgotten.

Memorial Day stands as a powerful testament to the unwavering dedication and sacrifice of the men and women who have laid down their lives in service to the United States. From its humble origins as Decoration Day to its evolution into a national holiday of remembrance, this solemn occasion holds deep meaning for Americans across the country. As we gather each year to honor the fallen, we ensure that their memory lives on, and their contributions to our nation are cherished. Memorial Day serves as a poignant reminder of the true cost of freedom and an enduring call to honor the brave men and women who have made the ultimate sacrifice in defense of liberty.

Independence Day - Celebrating the Spirit of Freedom

(July 4th)

Independence Day, also known as the Fourth of July, holds a special place in the hearts of Americans as a day of great national pride and celebration. In this chapter, we delve into the rich history, vibrant traditions, and profound significance of Independence Day. From the declaration that sparked a revolution to the modern-day festivities that unite a nation, we explore the enduring spirit of freedom that is at the core of this beloved holiday.

The Birth of a Nation:
Independence Day commemorates the historic moment on July 4, 1776, when the Continental Congress adopted the Declaration of Independence, officially declaring the American colonies' separation from Great Britain. This bold and revolutionary act laid the foundation for the birth of a new nation, founded on the principles of liberty, equality, and self-governance. The signing of the Declaration of Independence marked a pivotal turning point in American history and set the stage for the arduous journey towards independence.

The Flames of Revolution:
To understand the significance of Independence Day, one must reflect on the events that led to the American Revolution. The colonists' discontent with British rule, rooted in grievances over taxation, representation, and the infringement of their rights, ignited a fiery passion for freedom. The call for independence resonated throughout the colonies, as patriots rallied behind the vision of a self-governing nation free from British tyranny.

The flames of revolution burned bright, fueled by the ideals of liberty and the determination to forge a new path.

A Declaration of Freedom:
The Declaration of Independence, authored primarily by Thomas Jefferson, stands as a seminal document in American history. It boldly proclaimed the inherent rights of all individuals and declared that governments derive their power from the consent of the governed. The stirring words of the Declaration resonated with the hearts of the American people, inspiring them to stand united against oppression and fight for their right to self-determination. Each year on Independence Day, we pay tribute to this monumental declaration that set the course for a nation's destiny.

Celebrating Freedom:
Independence Day is a celebration of the hard-fought freedom that Americans enjoy. From coast to coast, communities come alive with a spirit of patriotism and unity. Fireworks illuminate the night sky, casting a kaleidoscope of colors that symbolize the vibrant diversity of the nation. Parades fill the streets, featuring marching bands, floats adorned with red, white, and blue, and displays of American pride. Barbecues and picnics bring families and friends together, as the tantalizing aroma of grilled favorites fills the air. It is a day of laughter, joy, and reflection on the liberties that were won through sacrifice and perseverance.

Honoring American Values:
Independence Day serves as a reminder of the core values upon which the United States was founded. It is a time to reflect on the principles of liberty, equality, and justice that define the nation's identity. Americans embrace the ideals of freedom of speech, religious freedom, and the pursuit of happiness, recognizing the ongoing journey to uphold these principles for all citizens. It is a day to express gratitude for the men and women who have served in the armed forces, protecting the nation's freedom and preserving the legacy of independence.

Looking Towards the Future:
As we celebrate Independence Day, we not only honor the past but also look towards the future. The day serves as a reminder of the responsibility to uphold the principles upon which the nation was built. It is a call to engage in active citizenship, to participate in the democratic process, and to contribute to the ongoing pursuit of a more perfect union. Independence Day inspires Americans to embrace their role as custodians of freedom, ensuring that the torch of liberty continues to burn brightly for generations to come.

Independence Day is more than just a holiday; it is a celebration of the indomitable spirit that shaped a nation. It is a day to honor the bravery and sacrifices of those who fought for independence, to reflect on the values that define the United States, and to come together as a nation united under the banner of freedom. From the momentous signing of the Declaration of Independence to the modern-day festivities that light up the skies, Independence Day embodies the unwavering spirit of liberty and the enduring pursuit of a more inclusive and equitable society.

Juneteenth - Emancipation and the Celebration of Freedom

(June 19th)

Juneteenth holds a special place in American history as a holiday that commemorates the emancipation of enslaved African Americans and celebrates the enduring spirit of freedom. In this chapter, we delve into the compelling story behind Juneteenth, exploring its origins, historical significance, and the vibrant traditions that surround this remarkable day of remembrance and joy.

The Legacy of Slavery:
To understand the significance of Juneteenth, one must confront the dark legacy of slavery in the United States. For centuries, millions of African men, women, and children endured unimaginable suffering and were subjected to the chains of bondage. Their forced labor and oppression were integral to the economic growth of the nation, yet their humanity and dignity were systematically denied.

Emancipation Proclamation:
The Emancipation Proclamation, issued by President Abraham Lincoln on January 1, 1863, served as a beacon of hope for those longing for freedom. It declared that all enslaved people within Confederate territories were to be set free. However, the proclamation's impact was limited by the realities of the ongoing Civil War and the resistance of slaveholding states. Many enslaved individuals remained in bondage even after the proclamation was issued.

The Arrival of Freedom:
It was on June 19, 1865, that the long-awaited news of emancipation reached the enslaved African Americans in Texas. Union General Gordon Granger arrived in Galveston, Texas, and delivered General Order No. 3, which proclaimed the freedom of

all enslaved people in accordance with the Emancipation Proclamation. This momentous announcement marked the beginning of a new era for those who had endured the horrors of slavery.

Juneteenth: A Celebration of Freedom:
Juneteenth, also known as Emancipation Day or Freedom Day, emerged as a day of celebration and remembrance. African Americans embraced this date as a symbol of their liberation and resilience in the face of immense adversity. The first Juneteenth celebrations centered around communal gatherings, music, prayer, and the sharing of stories that reflected the collective journey towards freedom.

Traditions and Customs:
Juneteenth is characterized by a range of traditions and customs that pay homage to African American heritage and highlight the importance of freedom. Community gatherings and parades fill the streets, with vibrant displays of African attire, music, dance, and performances. The red drink known as "Juneteenth Punch" symbolizes the bloodshed and resilience of African ancestors. Barbecues, picnics, and feasts bring families and friends together, fostering a sense of unity and joy.

Preserving History and Nurturing Identity:
Juneteenth serves as a powerful reminder of the struggles and triumphs in the journey towards equality and justice. It is a day to honor the sacrifices of those who fought for freedom, to acknowledge the contributions of African Americans to the fabric of American society, and to educate future generations about the realities of the nation's history. Through historical reenactments, educational programs, and cultural exhibitions, communities embrace the responsibility of preserving and sharing the stories that shape their identity.

Recognition and Significance:
The movement to recognize Juneteenth as a national holiday gained momentum in the latter half of the 20th century and early 21st century. Various organizations and individuals, including community leaders, activists, and lawmakers, advocated for its official recognition. They highlighted the importance of acknowledging Juneteenth as a pivotal moment in American history and an opportunity to promote unity, education, and healing.

Efforts to establish Juneteenth as a federal holiday intensified in recent years. In 2020, against the backdrop of nationwide protests against racial injustice and inequality, there was renewed focus on recognizing Juneteenth as a significant milestone in the fight for civil rights. The growing awareness and support for Juneteenth culminated in the U.S.

House of Representatives passing the Juneteenth National Independence Day Act on June 16, 2021, by a unanimous vote. The U.S. Senate followed suit, passing the bill the next day, and it was subsequently signed into law by President Joe Biden on June 17, 2021.

The establishment of Juneteenth as a federal holiday represents a milestone in the recognition of African American history and the ongoing pursuit of racial equality. It provides an opportunity for Americans to commemorate the emancipation of enslaved African Americans, reflect on the struggles and achievements of Black individuals and communities, and promote the values of freedom, justice, and equality for all.

Looking Ahead:
As Juneteenth continues to gain recognition and significance across the nation, it serves as a call to action. It prompts individuals and communities to confront the ongoing struggles for racial equality and justice, to engage in conversations about systemic racism, and to work collectively towards a future where freedom and opportunity are truly accessible to all.

Juneteenth stands as a testament to the indomitable spirit of African Americans and their unwavering pursuit of freedom. It is a day to honor the journey from enslavement to emancipation, to celebrate the rich heritage and contributions of African Americans, and to strive for a more just and equitable society. Let us embrace Juneteenth as a powerful reminder of the resilience of the human spirit and a catalyst for meaningful change.

Labor Day - Honoring the American Worker

(First Monday in September)

Labor Day stands as a tribute to the tireless contributions and achievements of the American workforce. In this chapter, we delve into the fascinating history, significance, and traditions surrounding Labor Day. From its origins in the labor movement to its modern-day observance as a national holiday, we explore the profound impact of this annual celebration of American workers.

Origins of the Labor Movement:
The seeds of Labor Day can be traced back to the Industrial Revolution, a transformative era marked by rapid industrialization and the rise of factories and manufacturing. As industrialization progressed, workers faced long hours, grueling conditions, and meager wages. In response, labor unions emerged as a collective voice for workers, advocating for better working conditions, fair wages, and improved rights. The labor movement gained momentum, fueled by strikes, protests, and the unwavering determination of workers to secure their rights.

A Day of Tribute:
Labor Day emerged as a result of the labor movement's efforts to recognize the invaluable contributions of the American workforce. The first Labor Day parade took place on September 5, 1882, in New York City, organized by the Central Labor Union. It served as a platform for workers to demonstrate solidarity and advocate for their rights. Inspired by this initial event, other cities soon followed suit, and the idea of a national holiday to honor workers gained traction.

Official Recognition and Legislation:
The growing momentum behind the labor movement and the significance of Labor Day led to its official recognition. On June 28, 1894, President Grover Cleveland signed a

law designating the first Monday in September as Labor Day, making it a national holiday. This recognition by the federal government served as a validation of the labor movement's goals and a testament to the importance of the American worker.

Celebrating American Workers:
Labor Day is a day of celebration and appreciation for the contributions of American workers. It is an occasion to recognize the dedication, resilience, and ingenuity of those who contribute to the nation's prosperity. Communities across the country engage in various traditions and activities to honor workers. Parades fill the streets, featuring floats representing different industries and labor unions. Workers proudly march alongside their colleagues, showcasing their skills and craftsmanship. Picnics, barbecues, and recreational activities bring families and friends together, providing a moment of relaxation and enjoyment.

The End of Summer:
Labor Day also marks the unofficial end of summer and the transition into the fall season. It provides an opportunity for individuals to gather with loved ones, enjoy the outdoors, and reflect on the achievements of the year thus far. Many people take advantage of the long weekend to travel, embark on one last summer adventure, or simply unwind and recharge before the demands of the coming months.

Impact and Legacy:
Labor Day's significance extends beyond its role as a national holiday. It serves as a reminder of the ongoing struggles and victories of the labor movement and the continuous fight for workers' rights and fair treatment. The achievements of the labor movement, such as the establishment of minimum wage laws, workplace safety regulations, and the fight against discrimination, have shaped the modern labor landscape. Labor Day is a testament to the collective power of workers and a call to maintain the progress achieved while advocating for further improvements.

Looking Ahead:
As we celebrate Labor Day, we honor the accomplishments of the past while looking towards the future. It is a day to recognize the ever-evolving nature of work and the challenges faced by the modern workforce. The rapid pace of technological advancement and the changing dynamics of the global economy present new opportunities and complexities for workers. Labor Day serves as a reminder to adapt, innovate, and continue advocating for the rights and well-being of all workers.

Labor Day stands as a testament to the unwavering dedication and hard work of the American worker. It is a day to honor the achievements of the labor movement, reflect on the progress made in securing workers' rights, and celebrate the contributions of individuals from all walks of life. As we gather with loved ones, participate in parades, and enjoy the festivities, let us remember the profound impact of labor in shaping the nation's history and look forward to a future where the labor force is empowered, respected, and thriving.

Columbus Day - Exploration, Controversy, and Commemoration

(Second Monday in October)

Columbus Day has long been a fixture on the American calendar, commemorating Christopher Columbus's historic voyage to the Americas in 1492. In this chapter, we embark on a journey to unravel the complex history and evolving significance of Columbus Day. We explore the exploration and impact of Christopher Columbus, the controversies surrounding his legacy, and the various perspectives on this controversial holiday.

Voyages of Exploration:
Christopher Columbus, an Italian explorer commissioned by the Catholic Monarchs of Spain, embarked on his ambitious expedition in search of a western route to Asia. On October 12, 1492, he made landfall in the Caribbean, unknowingly opening the door to a new era of exploration, colonization, and cultural exchange between the Old World and the New.

Legacy and Historical Context:
Columbus's voyages had far-reaching consequences, sparking a period of European exploration and the eventual colonization of the Americas. While celebrated as a pivotal moment in history, Columbus's arrival also initiated the displacement, subjugation, and exploitation of Indigenous peoples across the continents. The impact of his actions and the subsequent colonization of the Americas remain subjects of debate and introspection.

Evolution of Columbus Day:
The observance of Columbus Day in the United States can be traced back to the late 19th century. Italian Americans, seeking recognition for their contributions to American

society, advocated for a holiday honoring Columbus, who was of Italian descent. In 1892, on the 400th anniversary of Columbus's arrival, President Benjamin Harrison proclaimed Columbus Day as a one-time national celebration. Over time, it became an annual observance, with Italian American communities leading the way in commemorating their cultural heritage and honoring Columbus's legacy.

Controversies and Criticisms:
As societal awareness grew, so did criticisms of Columbus's actions and the celebration of Columbus Day. Indigenous activists and their allies began to challenge the holiday, pointing to the violence, forced labor, and devastation brought upon Indigenous populations as a result of European colonization. The historical context surrounding Columbus's arrival and the subsequent impact on Native Americans have sparked debates about the appropriateness of honoring him as a figure of celebration.

Alternatives and Redefinition:
In response to the controversies surrounding Columbus Day, alternative observances have emerged. Some communities have replaced Columbus Day with Indigenous Peoples' Day, recognizing and celebrating the rich cultures, contributions, and resilience of Native American and Indigenous communities. This shift aims to foster a more inclusive narrative, acknowledging the historical experiences and ongoing struggles of Indigenous peoples.

Education and Dialogue:
The controversies surrounding Columbus Day have underscored the importance of education and dialogue about the true history of the Americas and the legacies of colonization. It is crucial to critically examine historical narratives, promote Indigenous perspectives, and engage in honest conversations about the complexities of history and the ongoing impacts of colonialism. By doing so, we can foster a more inclusive understanding of the past and work towards reconciliation and justice.

Reflections and Moving Forward:
As Columbus Day continues to be a topic of debate and introspection, it serves as a reminder of the power of collective reflection and societal evolution. It prompts us to question traditional narratives, acknowledge historical complexities, and strive for a more inclusive and equitable future. By reevaluating our commemorative practices, engaging in meaningful dialogue, and uplifting marginalized voices, we can reshape the narrative and contribute to a more just and inclusive society.

Columbus Day stands at a crossroads, caught between celebration and criticism, exploration and exploitation, triumph and tragedy. As we navigate the complexities of this holiday, let us reflect on the history it represents, acknowledge the ongoing struggles for justice and reconciliation, and commit ourselves to creating a future that values diversity, inclusivity, and the shared humanity of all peoples. By doing so, we can transform Columbus Day into a catalyst for reflection, learning, and positive change.

29

Indigenous Peoples Day - Honoring Native Histories, Resilience, and Cultures

(Second Monday in October)

Indigenous Peoples Day represents a significant shift in the recognition and celebration of Native American and Indigenous communities in the United States. In this chapter, we explore the origins, significance, and growing movement behind Indigenous Peoples Day. We delve into the histories, cultures, and ongoing struggles of Indigenous peoples, highlighting the importance of honoring their rich legacies and fostering understanding and respect.

A Legacy of Resilience:
Indigenous peoples have inhabited the lands now known as the United States for thousands of years, cultivating diverse cultures, languages, and traditions that are deeply intertwined with the land. However, the arrival of European colonizers led to centuries of dispossession, forced assimilation, and marginalization of Native American and Indigenous communities. Despite these immense challenges, Indigenous peoples have demonstrated remarkable resilience, preserving their cultures, languages, and spiritual traditions.

The Emergence of Indigenous Peoples Day:
The call for the recognition of Indigenous Peoples Day emerged in the late 20th century as a response to the historical inaccuracies and misrepresentations embedded in the celebration of Columbus Day. Activists, Indigenous leaders, and their allies began advocating for a holiday that would honor the contributions, resilience, and ongoing struggles of Native American and Indigenous communities. This movement sought to shift the narrative, challenge colonial legacies, and foster a more accurate understanding of American history.

The First Celebrations:
The first official observances of Indigenous Peoples Day occurred in the early 1990s. Cities and communities across the United States, inspired by the vision and activism of Indigenous leaders, adopted resolutions to replace or augment Columbus Day with Indigenous Peoples Day. These early celebrations centered around cultural events, educational programs, and community gatherings that highlighted Indigenous histories, art, music, and dance.

Recognition and Symbolism:
Indigenous Peoples Day serves as a platform to honor and recognize the diverse cultures, histories, and contributions of Native American and Indigenous communities. It acknowledges the deep connections between Indigenous peoples and the lands they have inhabited since time immemorial. By elevating Indigenous voices and perspectives, the holiday aims to promote understanding, challenge stereotypes, and foster a more inclusive society.

Cultural Preservation and Revitalization:
Indigenous Peoples Day is an opportunity to celebrate the resilience and perseverance of Indigenous cultures. It provides a platform for Indigenous artists, performers, and storytellers to share their traditions, languages, and arts with broader audiences. Efforts to preserve and revitalize Indigenous languages, traditional ecological knowledge, and artistic practices are essential components of the holiday, ensuring that future generations can continue to connect with their ancestral roots.

Reckoning with Historical Injustices:
Indigenous Peoples Day also invites reflection and reckoning with the historical injustices inflicted upon Native American and Indigenous communities. It encourages individuals and communities to confront the legacies of colonization, land dispossession, forced assimilation, and systemic oppression. By acknowledging these painful truths, we can work towards healing, reconciliation, and justice.

Education and Awareness:
Education plays a crucial role in the observance of Indigenous Peoples Day. Schools, universities, museums, and cultural institutions have embraced the opportunity to provide accurate and comprehensive education about Native American and Indigenous histories. This includes highlighting the contributions of Indigenous peoples to diverse fields, challenging stereotypes, and nurturing a more empathetic understanding of their experiences.

The Future of Indigenous Peoples Day:

As the movement to recognize Indigenous Peoples Day continues to gain momentum, more cities, states, and institutions are adopting the holiday. The growing acceptance of Indigenous Peoples Day reflects an evolving understanding of history and a commitment to rectifying past injustices. It serves as a reminder that the story of the United States is multifaceted, encompassing the rich tapestry of Native American and Indigenous cultures.

Indigenous Peoples Day is a pivotal moment in the ongoing journey towards recognizing and honoring the histories, cultures, and contributions of Native American and Indigenous communities. It is a day to celebrate resilience, challenge historical inaccuracies, and foster understanding and respect. By embracing the spirit of Indigenous Peoples Day, we can create a society that values and uplifts the voices and experiences of Indigenous peoples, forging a path towards a more inclusive and equitable future.

Veterans Day - Honoring Service, Sacrifice, and Patriotism

(November 11th)

Veterans Day holds a special place in the hearts of Americans as a time to honor and express gratitude to the men and women who have served in the United States armed forces. In this chapter, we delve into the history, significance, and commemorative traditions associated with Veterans Day. We explore the experiences of veterans, the evolution of this important holiday, and the ways in which we can collectively honor and support those who have bravely defended our nation.

Origins and Armistice Day:
The roots of Veterans Day can be traced back to the end of World War I, when an armistice was signed on November 11, 1918, marking the cessation of hostilities on the Western Front. This armistice became the catalyst for the observance of Armistice Day, a holiday that recognized the sacrifices made by the soldiers who fought in the Great War. It was a solemn day of remembrance and gratitude.

Evolution into Veterans Day:
In 1954, after the end of World War II and the Korean War, Armistice Day was officially renamed Veterans Day to encompass all veterans who had served in the U.S. military. The renaming of the holiday reflected the nation's desire to honor the contributions and sacrifices of veterans from all wars and conflicts, acknowledging that the commitment to defend the nation extends far beyond a single moment in history.

Honoring Service and Sacrifice:
Veterans Day serves as a solemn reminder of the dedication and bravery exhibited by those who have served in the armed forces. It is a time to reflect on the sacrifices made by veterans and their families, recognizing the physical and emotional toll that military

service can exact. The holiday provides an opportunity to express gratitude for their selflessness and unwavering commitment to protecting our nation and its values.

Ceremonies and Commemorative Practices:
Across the country, communities come together to honor veterans through various ceremonies and commemorative practices. Parades, wreath-laying ceremonies, and memorial services are held to pay tribute to those who have served. These events serve as reminders of the collective responsibility to support and care for veterans, as well as opportunities to connect with and learn from their experiences.

Supporting Veterans and Their Transition:
Veterans Day is not only a time for reflection and remembrance but also an opportunity to provide support and resources to veterans. Transitioning from military service to civilian life can be challenging, and it is important to ensure that veterans have access to the care, benefits, and opportunities they deserve. Efforts to address the physical and mental health needs of veterans, expand educational and job training opportunities, and strengthen community support networks are crucial to honoring their service beyond a single day.

Recognizing Diversity and Women Veterans:
Veterans Day is an occasion to acknowledge the diversity of those who have served. It is essential to recognize the contributions and sacrifices made by women veterans, who have played vital roles in the armed forces throughout history. Their experiences and perspectives enrich the narrative of military service and underscore the importance of inclusivity and gender equality within the veteran community.

Educating Future Generations:
As the number of living veterans from World War II and the Korean War decreases, it becomes increasingly important to educate future generations about the significance of Veterans Day and the importance of honoring those who have served. Educational programs, classroom activities, and community initiatives can help instill an understanding of the sacrifices made by veterans and cultivate a sense of gratitude and respect for their service.

Renewed Commitment and Continued Support:
While Veterans Day offers a dedicated moment to honor veterans, it is imperative that our commitment to supporting them extends beyond a single day. Promoting access to healthcare, mental health services, educational opportunities, employment assistance, and housing resources are ongoing efforts that demonstrate our collective gratitude and commitment to those who have served.

Veterans Day stands as a powerful reminder of the sacrifices, bravery, and unwavering dedication of the men and women who have served in the U.S. armed forces. It is a day to honor their contributions, recognize their experiences, and express our gratitude for their selflessness. By coming together as a nation, we can ensure that veterans are not forgotten and that their service and sacrifices are valued and appreciated. Veterans Day serves as a beacon of remembrance, unity, and support, illuminating the path toward a more compassionate and grateful society.

Thanksgiving Day - A Time for Gratitude and Unity

(Fourth Thursday in November)

Thanksgiving Day holds a special place in the hearts and homes of Americans as a time of gratitude, togetherness, and reflection. In this chapter, we delve into the history, traditions, and meaning behind this beloved holiday. From its humble beginnings as a harvest feast shared by Pilgrims and Native Americans to its modern-day celebration, Thanksgiving has evolved into a cherished national observance that transcends cultural and religious boundaries.

Origins and the Pilgrim Story:
The roots of Thanksgiving can be traced back to the early 17th century when a group of English Pilgrims known as the Pilgrims settled in Plymouth, Massachusetts, after a long and arduous journey across the Atlantic Ocean. Faced with a harsh and unfamiliar environment, they relied on the assistance and guidance of the Wampanoag Native Americans, who taught them essential survival skills and helped forge a spirit of cooperation and friendship.

The First Thanksgiving:
In the autumn of 1621, after the Pilgrims had successfully harvested their first crops, they held a celebratory feast to express gratitude for the blessings of the harvest season. This historic gathering, known as the First Thanksgiving, was a communal event that brought together the Pilgrims and Wampanoag people in a spirit of unity and appreciation. It marked a significant moment of cultural exchange and mutual respect.

Evolution of Thanksgiving:
Throughout the years, Thanksgiving continued to be observed in various forms and on different dates. It wasn't until 1863, during the height of the Civil War, that President

Abraham Lincoln proclaimed Thanksgiving as a national holiday to be celebrated on the fourth Thursday of November. Lincoln's intention was to foster unity and healing in a divided nation, encouraging Americans to set aside their differences and come together in gratitude.

Traditions and Celebrations:
Thanksgiving has evolved into a holiday characterized by cherished traditions and customs. Families and friends gather around the dining table to share a bountiful meal that typically includes roasted turkey, stuffing, cranberry sauce, and pumpkin pie. The aroma of these dishes fills the air as loved ones engage in heartfelt conversations, laughter, and expressions of gratitude. It is a time to pause, reflect, and appreciate the blessings in our lives.

Macy's Thanksgiving Day Parade:
One iconic aspect of Thanksgiving is the Macy's Thanksgiving Day Parade, a spectacle that has captivated audiences since its inception in 1924. The parade, featuring larger-than-life helium balloons, floats, marching bands, and performances, has become a beloved tradition that signals the official start of the holiday season. Millions of viewers tune in from their homes, while thousands brave the cold streets of New York City to witness the magic firsthand.

Giving Thanks and Acts of Kindness:
Thanksgiving not only serves as a time for personal reflection but also as an opportunity to extend kindness and generosity to others. Many individuals and communities engage in charitable acts, volunteering at food banks, organizing donation drives, and reaching out to those in need. These acts of service exemplify the spirit of Thanksgiving and remind us of the importance of compassion and empathy.

Cultural and Regional Variations:
While Thanksgiving is widely celebrated throughout the United States, there are variations in how it is observed across different regions and cultural communities. Some families incorporate their own cultural traditions and dishes into the holiday meal, adding a unique flair to the festivities. Native American communities also embrace the holiday, intertwining their own cultural practices and expressions of gratitude with the historical significance of the Pilgrim-Wampanoag encounter.

Reflection and Gratitude in the Modern Age:
In today's fast-paced and interconnected world, Thanksgiving serves as a reminder to slow down, disconnect from technology, and embrace the company of loved ones. It

encourages us to reflect on the blessings in our lives, express gratitude for the simple joys, and cultivate a spirit of thankfulness that extends beyond a single day.

Thanksgiving Day stands as a testament to the power of gratitude, unity, and shared humanity. It reminds us to pause, reflect, and appreciate the abundance in our lives while fostering a sense of togetherness and empathy. Through the centuries, Thanksgiving has evolved, carrying with it the stories of the Pilgrims, the spirit of cultural exchange, and the importance of giving thanks. As families and communities gather around the table, the essence of Thanksgiving shines through, reminding us to cherish the blessings we have and extend kindness to others.

Christmas Day - Celebrating the Joy of the Season

(December 25th)

Christmas Day, with its timeless traditions and festive spirit, holds a special place in the hearts of Americans. In this chapter, we explore the rich history, customs, and significance of this beloved holiday. From religious observances to secular celebrations, Christmas has become a cherished time of joy, giving, and togetherness.

The Birth of Christmas:
At the heart of Christmas lies the celebration of the birth of Jesus Christ, the central figure of Christianity. With roots in the early Christian Church, the holiday gained prominence through the centuries, blending religious beliefs with cultural customs and pagan traditions. In the United States, Christmas has evolved into a unique blend of religious observance and secular festivities.

Religious Observances:
For millions of Americans, Christmas holds deep religious significance. Churches come alive with vibrant displays, candlelight services, and the retelling of the Nativity story. The faithful gather to sing hymns, pray, and reflect on the profound message of hope and redemption that Christmas represents. From midnight Mass to the joyous sounds of caroling, these observances provide spiritual nourishment and a sense of community.

Secular Traditions:
Beyond the religious observances, Christmas has also become a time for secular customs that bring joy and merriment to people of all backgrounds. The exchange of

gifts, inspired by the biblical tale of the Magi, symbolizes the spirit of giving and generosity. Festive decorations adorn homes and public spaces, with colorful lights, wreaths, and Christmas trees becoming iconic symbols of the season. Families come together to decorate the tree, hang stockings, and create a warm and inviting atmosphere.

Santa Claus and the Spirit of Giving:
Central to the secular celebration of Christmas is the beloved figure of Santa Claus. Inspired by the historical figure of Saint Nicholas, Santa Claus embodies the spirit of giving and joy. Children eagerly await his arrival, leaving out milk and cookies in anticipation of his visit. The tradition of Santa Claus has transcended cultures and borders, symbolizing the universal spirit of kindness and generosity.

Holiday Treats and Culinary Delights:
Christmas is also a time for indulging in delicious treats and culinary delights. Traditional dishes vary from region to region, reflecting the diverse cultural backgrounds of the American people. From roast turkey to honey-glazed ham, from gingerbread houses to fruitcakes, the holiday table is filled with an abundance of flavors and aromas that evoke memories and create a sense of comfort and nostalgia.

Carols and Music:
The sounds of Christmas fill the air, bringing joy and warmth to the holiday season. Christmas carols, both traditional hymns and contemporary songs, echo through churches, shopping centers, and homes. Choral performances, concerts, and sing-alongs uplift spirits and create a sense of shared celebration. Music has the power to evoke emotions and foster a sense of unity, making it an integral part of the Christmas experience.

Family Traditions and Bonding:
Christmas is a time for families to come together, creating cherished memories and fostering deep connections. It is a time for reunions, laughter, and heartfelt conversations. Whether through the exchanging of gifts, the preparation of a special meal, or the reading of timeless stories, families forge traditions that are passed down through generations. These traditions strengthen the bond of family and create a sense of belonging.

Holiday Spirit and Acts of Kindness:
Christmas also serves as a reminder of the importance of compassion and goodwill towards others. Many embrace the holiday spirit by engaging in acts of kindness and charitable giving. Whether it's donating to food drives, volunteering at homeless

shelters, or reaching out to those in need, these acts embody the true meaning of Christmas - spreading love and bringing joy to others.

Reflection and Renewal:
In the midst of the holiday hustle and bustle, Christmas also provides an opportunity for reflection and renewal. It is a time to pause and take stock of the year gone by, to express gratitude for the blessings received, and to set intentions for the year ahead. The end of the calendar year coinciding with Christmas prompts individuals to reflect on personal growth, values, and aspirations.

Christmas Day, with its blend of religious and secular traditions, holds a special place in the hearts of Americans. It is a time of joy, giving, and togetherness, where families and communities come together to celebrate and share in the holiday spirit. Whether through religious observances, festive customs, or acts of kindness, Christmas carries a message of hope, love, and unity. As the year comes to a close, Christmas Day offers a moment of reflection and renewal, reminding us of the importance of faith, family, and the bonds that connect us all.

Part 2: Regional and Cultural Holidays

Mardi Gras - Revelry, Tradition, and Cultural Extravaganza

(typically falls in February)

Mardi Gras, the lively and exuberant carnival season celebrated in various parts of the United States, holds a special place in American culture. In this chapter, we delve into the vibrant history, traditions, and festivities that make Mardi Gras a beloved and highly anticipated event. From the grand parades to the elaborate costumes, Mardi Gras showcases the spirit of revelry and community.

Origins and Cultural Influences:
The origins of Mardi Gras can be traced back to ancient pagan celebrations that marked the transition from winter to spring. Over time, these pagan rituals merged with Christian traditions, particularly the observance of Lent. Today, Mardi Gras is celebrated predominantly in areas with French and Spanish heritage, such as New Orleans, Louisiana, and Mobile, Alabama, where it has become deeply ingrained in the local culture.

New Orleans: The Epicenter of Mardi Gras:
New Orleans, Louisiana, is synonymous with Mardi Gras, known for its elaborate parades, vibrant costumes, and lively street parties. The city's unique blend of French, Spanish, African, and Caribbean influences has shaped its distinctive Mardi Gras celebrations. The festivities kick off in January and culminate on Fat Tuesday, the day before Ash Wednesday and the beginning of the Lenten season.

Krewes and Parades:
Central to Mardi Gras are the krewes, social organizations that plan and host parades and balls during the carnival season. Each krewe has its own theme, floats, and masked riders who toss trinkets, known as "throws," to the cheering crowds. The parades are a spectacle of creativity, featuring intricately designed floats, marching bands, and flamboyant costumes that showcase the artistic spirit of Mardi Gras.

Costumes and Masks:
Mardi Gras is a time for revelers to don elaborate costumes and masks, adding to the festive atmosphere. The costumes range from historical and mythical characters to vibrant, sequined ensembles that reflect the individual's creativity and imagination. Masks, often adorned with feathers, sequins, and intricate designs, allow participants to embrace anonymity and fully immerse themselves in the spirit of celebration.

Beads and Throws:
Beads have become synonymous with Mardi Gras, symbolizing the spirit of generosity and camaraderie. As parade floats pass by, masked riders shower the crowds with beads, plush toys, doubloons (collectible coins), and other throws. Catching these throws has become a cherished tradition, with attendees eagerly vying for the colorful trinkets as tokens of good luck and remembrance.

King Cakes and Culinary Delights:
No Mardi Gras celebration is complete without indulging in the delectable delights associated with the season. King cakes, sweet and festive pastries adorned with colorful icing and sugar crystals, take center stage. These cakes are baked with a hidden plastic baby figurine inside, symbolizing luck and prosperity for the person who finds it. Additionally, traditional New Orleans cuisine, such as gumbo, jambalaya, and beignets, tantalize the taste buds of locals and visitors alike.

Music and Jazz:
Mardi Gras is synonymous with the vibrant sounds of jazz music, which permeate the streets of New Orleans during the carnival season. Jazz bands, marching bands, and brass ensembles fill the air with their lively tunes, creating an energetic and infectious atmosphere. The rhythmic beats and soulful melodies of jazz embody the celebratory spirit of Mardi Gras, inspiring people to dance, sing, and revel in the moment.

Community and Social Impact:
Mardi Gras holds significant social and economic importance for the communities that celebrate it. The festival brings people from all walks of life together, fostering a sense of unity and shared celebration. Beyond its cultural significance, Mardi Gras also provides an economic boost to local businesses, hotels, restaurants, and tourism, attracting visitors from around the world.

Mardi Gras, with its colorful parades, lively music, elaborate costumes, and vibrant traditions, embodies the spirit of celebration and community. From its ancient origins to the modern-day festivities in New Orleans and other regions, Mardi Gras showcases the rich tapestry of American culture. This annual extravaganza allows people to let loose, embrace joy, and immerse themselves in the magic of this cherished holiday. As the saying goes, "Laissez les bons temps rouler!" - Let the good times roll!

45

St. Patrick's Day - Irish Heritage and Festive Merriment

(March 17th)

St. Patrick's Day, observed annually on March 17th, is a celebration of Irish culture and heritage that has become widely embraced in the United States. In this chapter, we delve into the rich history, traditions, and festivities associated with St. Patrick's Day. From the iconic parades to the wearing of green, this holiday brings people together to honor the patron saint of Ireland and to revel in the joyous spirit of the occasion.

Early Origins:
St. Patrick's Day commemorates the life and work of Saint Patrick, the patron saint of Ireland. Born in Britain in the 4th century, Patrick was captured by Irish raiders and brought to Ireland as a slave. After escaping and returning to his homeland, he later returned to Ireland as a missionary, spreading Christianity and establishing churches. St. Patrick's Day initially began as a religious observance, marking the date of his death.

Arrival of St. Patrick's Day in the United States:
The celebration of St. Patrick's Day in the United States can be traced back to the early 18th century when Irish immigrants began to arrive in significant numbers. They brought with them their customs, including the celebration of their patron saint's feast day. Initially, the holiday was primarily observed within Irish communities, but over time it gained popularity and acceptance among people of various backgrounds.

Parades and Festivities:

One of the most iconic aspects of St. Patrick's Day in the United States is the grand parades held in cities across the country. The first St. Patrick's Day parade took place in New York City in 1762 and has since become an annual tradition. These parades feature vibrant floats, marching bands, bagpipers, and participants dressed in green. People line the streets, donning green attire, and join in the festivities, creating a spectacle of joy and celebration.

Wearing of the Green:
On St. Patrick's Day, it is customary to wear green clothing and accessories. The practice stems from the belief that wearing green makes one invisible to mischievous leprechauns and brings good luck. People proudly display their Irish heritage by adorning themselves in green attire, hats, and accessories, creating a sea of green throughout the day's festivities.

Traditional Irish Music and Dance:
Music and dance play a vital role in St. Patrick's Day celebrations. Traditional Irish music, characterized by lively jigs, reels, and ballads, fills the air as musicians showcase their talent. Irish step dancing, with its intricate footwork and lively rhythms, captivates audiences and adds to the festive atmosphere. Many St. Patrick's Day events feature performances by Irish musicians and dancers, inviting everyone to join in the merriment.

Culinary Delights:
No St. Patrick's Day celebration would be complete without indulging in traditional Irish cuisine. Corned beef and cabbage, a staple dish associated with the holiday, is often enjoyed alongside soda bread, Irish stew, and colcannon (a mixture of potatoes and cabbage or kale). Pubs and restaurants serve up pints of Guinness, Ireland's famous stout, as well as other Irish-inspired beverages.

Symbols and Traditions:
St. Patrick's Day is rich in symbols and traditions. The shamrock, a three-leafed clover, is closely associated with St. Patrick and serves as a symbol of Ireland. It is believed that Patrick used the shamrock to explain the concept of the Holy Trinity. Additionally, the Celtic cross, Claddagh ring, and harp are symbols that represent Irish heritage and are often seen during St. Patrick's Day celebrations.

St. Patrick's Day is a cherished holiday in the United States, where people of all backgrounds come together to celebrate Irish culture and heritage. Through parades, music, dance, and culinary delights, this festive occasion honors the legacy of Saint Patrick and the contributions of the Irish community. It is a day filled with joy, camaraderie, and the wearing of green, as Americans embrace their inner Irish spirit and revel in the festive atmosphere. Sláinte! (Cheers!)

Diwali - The Festival of Lights and Cultural Celebration

(between mid-October to mid-November)

Diwali, also known as Deepavali, is one of the most significant festivals celebrated by Hindus, Sikhs, and Jains around the world. In this chapter, we explore the vibrant and joyous celebration of Diwali in the United States. From the origins and religious significance of the festival to the elaborate rituals, decorations, and culinary delights associated with it, Diwali brings communities together to illuminate the darkness with light and embrace the triumph of good over evil.

Origins and Religious Significance:
Diwali traces its origins back to ancient India and is rooted in Hindu mythology. The festival commemorates the return of Lord Rama, an incarnation of the Hindu god Vishnu, from exile after defeating the demon king Ravana. The lighting of lamps and fireworks symbolizes the triumph of light over darkness and the victory of righteousness over evil. Additionally, Diwali holds significance for Sikhs as it marks the release of their sixth Guru, Guru Hargobind, from captivity, and for Jains, it celebrates the attainment of moksha (liberation) by Mahavira, the last Jain Tirthankara.

Preparations and Decorations:
The preparations for Diwali begin weeks in advance, with families cleaning their homes and decorating them with vibrant colors, flowers, and intricate rangoli designs made of colored powders or rice. Clay diyas (lamps) are lit, illuminating the surroundings and creating a warm and welcoming ambiance. Decorative lights, lanterns, and strings of colorful electric bulbs adorn houses, temples, and public spaces, turning the entire community into a spectacle of radiance.

Prayers, Puja, and Festive Rituals:

Diwali is a time of spiritual reflection and worship. Families gather for puja (prayer) ceremonies, offering prayers to deities such as Lord Rama, Goddess Lakshmi (the goddess of wealth and prosperity), and Lord Ganesha (the remover of obstacles). Devotees perform aarti (rituals with lamps), chant mantras, and seek blessings for health, wealth, and happiness. Fireworks are set off to drive away evil spirits and create a joyous atmosphere of celebration.

Feasting and Culinary Delights:
Food plays a central role in Diwali celebrations. Families prepare a variety of traditional sweets and savory dishes to share with loved ones and offer to deities. Popular Diwali sweets include gulab jamun (fried milk dumplings soaked in syrup), jalebi (syrup-soaked deep-fried pretzels), and barfi (a sweet fudge-like confection). Savory delights like samosas, pakoras, and flavored rice dishes add to the culinary extravaganza. Diwali feasts bring families and communities together, fostering bonds of love and camaraderie.

Exchange of Gifts and Prayers for Prosperity:
Diwali is a time for exchanging gifts as a symbol of love and goodwill. Families and friends present each other with sweets, fruits, dry fruits, and decorative items. It is also common to give money or gold coins as a gesture of prosperity and good fortune. Business owners offer prayers for the success and prosperity of their enterprises, and people decorate their workplaces with colorful rangoli designs and flowers.

Community Celebrations and Cultural Programs:
In the United States, Diwali is celebrated with great enthusiasm by the Indian diaspora and embraced by people from diverse cultural backgrounds. Community organizations, temples, and cultural associations organize grand Diwali events, featuring music, dance performances, traditional plays, and art exhibitions. These festivities showcase the richness of Indian culture, allowing people to experience the vibrant traditions associated with Diwali.

Diwali in the United States is a time of joy, togetherness, and spiritual renewal. It is a celebration that transcends religious and cultural boundaries, bringing people from various backgrounds together to appreciate the beauty of lights, the significance of tradition, and the triumph of good over evil. As the festival of Diwali spreads its radiant glow across the nation, it illuminates hearts, fosters unity, and reminds everyone of the power of light and love in our lives.

Hanukkah - The Festival of Lights and Jewish Heritage

(varies each year based on the Hebrew calendar)

Hanukkah, also known as the Festival of Lights, holds a special place in the hearts of Jewish communities around the world. In this chapter, we delve into the rich history, religious significance, and cultural traditions associated with Hanukkah in the United States. From the lighting of the menorah to the joyous festivities and culinary delights, Hanukkah is a time for celebration, remembrance, and the triumph of light over darkness.

Origins and Religious Significance:
Hanukkah commemorates the miracle that occurred during the rededication of the Holy Temple in Jerusalem in the second century BCE. The story revolves around the Maccabees, a group of Jewish fighters who successfully revolted against the oppressive rule of the Seleucid Empire. The festival lasts for eight nights, representing the miraculous burning of the menorah (a seven-branched candelabrum) in the temple, even though there was only enough sacred oil to last for one day. Hanukkah serves as a reminder of the resilience, faith, and commitment to religious freedom.

Lighting the Menorah:
At the heart of Hanukkah celebrations is the lighting of the menorah. Each night, one additional candle is added to the menorah until all eight candles, plus the central one known as the shamash (helper), are lit. This ritual takes place at sundown, with families gathering around the menorah, reciting blessings, and singing traditional songs. The glow of the menorah symbolizes hope, unity, and the power of perseverance.

Playing Dreidel:

Dreidel, a spinning top with Hebrew letters on each side, is a beloved Hanukkah game. Family and friends gather to play this traditional game of chance, where participants bet with gelt (chocolate coins) or other small treats. The letters on the dreidel, Nun, Gimel, Hey, and Shin, stand for the phrase "Nes Gadol Haya Sham," meaning "A great miracle happened there." The game adds an element of fun and excitement to the festivities, creating lasting memories for all.

Hanukkah Foods:
Food is an integral part of Hanukkah celebrations, with special dishes and treats prepared to honor the holiday. The most iconic Hanukkah food is the crispy potato pancake known as latkes. These delicious treats are made from grated potatoes, onions, and eggs, fried until golden and served with applesauce or sour cream. Another beloved Hanukkah delicacy is sufganiyot, deep-fried jelly-filled doughnuts dusted with powdered sugar. These delectable treats symbolize the oil that miraculously burned in the temple.

Gift-Giving and Gelt:
In keeping with the spirit of joy and gratitude, gift-giving is a cherished tradition during Hanukkah. Families exchange presents, particularly focusing on gifts for children. In addition, gelt, which are chocolate coins wrapped in gold or silver foil, are given to children to celebrate the holiday. The act of giving gifts and gelt reinforces the importance of generosity and brings smiles to the faces of loved ones.

Community Celebrations:
Hanukkah is celebrated not only within the confines of homes but also within the wider Jewish community. Synagogues, Jewish community centers, and organizations host public menorah lightings, cultural performances, and festive gatherings. These community events foster a sense of belonging, unity, and shared pride in Jewish heritage. Hanukkah becomes a time for reconnecting with one's roots, strengthening bonds, and embracing the diversity of Jewish traditions.

Hanukkah Across America:
Throughout the United States, Hanukkah is celebrated with enthusiasm and vibrancy. Major cities, such as New York, Los Angeles, and Miami, host spectacular public menorah lightings, often accompanied by live music, dance performances, and festive activities. From bustling city streets to small towns, the glow of the menorah illuminates the spirit of Hanukkah, reminding Jews and non-Jews alike of the value of religious freedom and the importance of spreading light in a world that can sometimes be dark.

Hanukkah in the United States is a time of joy, togetherness, and celebration. From the lighting of the menorah to the playing of dreidel, the savoring of traditional foods, and the exchange of gifts, Hanukkah fills hearts with warmth and gratitude. It is a time to honor Jewish heritage, reflect on the lessons of resilience and freedom, and create cherished memories with loved ones. As the candles of the menorah illuminate homes and communities, Hanukkah reminds us all of the power of faith, hope, and the enduring light that guides us through life's challenges.

Eid al-Fitr - Celebrating the Festival of Breaking the Fast

(varies each year based on the Islamic lunar calendar)

Eid al-Fitr is a significant and joyous Islamic holiday that marks the end of Ramadan, a month-long period of fasting and spiritual reflection. In this chapter, we explore the traditions, customs, and cultural significance of Eid al-Fitr in the United States. From the early morning prayers to the festive gatherings and acts of charity, Eid al-Fitr is a time of renewal, gratitude, and community.

The Observance of Ramadan:
To truly appreciate the celebration of Eid al-Fitr, it is essential to understand the preceding month of Ramadan. Muslims around the world observe a daily fast from dawn to sunset, abstaining from food, drink, and other physical needs. This month is a time of increased devotion, self-reflection, and seeking closeness to Allah. Muslims strive to purify their souls, engage in charitable acts, and deepen their connection with the Quran.

The Sighting of the New Moon:
The exact date of Eid al-Fitr is determined by the sighting of the new moon, signaling the end of Ramadan. Islamic communities in the United States eagerly await the announcement from local Islamic organizations or the sighting of the moon by trustworthy individuals. This anticipation creates a sense of unity and shared excitement as Muslims prepare for the upcoming celebration.

The Day of Eid al-Fitr:

Eid al-Fitr begins with the congregational prayer known as Salat al-Eid, performed in mosques, prayer halls, or outdoor spaces. Muslims dress in their finest attire, often wearing traditional clothing, to mark the importance of the occasion. The prayer is led by an Imam, and attendees listen attentively to the sermon, which emphasizes gratitude, unity, and acts of compassion.

Festive Atmosphere and Community Celebrations:
Following the prayer, the atmosphere becomes festive and joyous as families and friends come together to celebrate Eid al-Fitr. Vibrant decorations, including colorful lights, banners, and ornaments, adorn homes and mosques. Islamic centers and community organizations host special events, including cultural performances, food bazaars, and activities for children. The celebrations are a testament to the diversity within the Muslim community and the shared values of unity and togetherness.

Traditional Foods and Sweet Delights:
Food plays a central role in Eid al-Fitr celebrations, with families preparing special dishes and delicacies to share with loved ones and guests. Each culture and region brings its own unique flavors and traditional recipes to the table. From savory dishes such as biryani, kebabs, and samosas to sweet treats like baklava, sheer khurma, and maamoul, the feasts during Eid al-Fitr are a culinary delight.

Acts of Charity and Giving:
Eid al-Fitr is a time of immense generosity and compassion. Muslims are encouraged to give to those in need through acts of charity, known as Zakat al-Fitr or Fitrah. This obligatory charitable donation ensures that even the less fortunate members of the community can partake in the festivities and experience joy during Eid al-Fitr. Donations are made to charitable organizations or directly to individuals, emphasizing the importance of sharing blessings and supporting one another.

Family Visits and Gift Exchanges:
Eid al-Fitr is also a time for reconnecting with family and friends. It is customary for Muslims to visit relatives and exchange heartfelt greetings and well-wishes. This practice strengthens familial bonds, fosters unity, and reinforces the importance of community ties. Additionally, it is common to exchange gifts, especially among children, as a way of expressing love and joy during this special celebration.

Eid al-Fitr in the United States:
Eid al-Fitr is celebrated with great enthusiasm and spirit in Muslim communities throughout the United States. Major cities such as New York, Chicago, Los Angeles, and Houston host grand gatherings and cultural events, attracting Muslims from diverse

backgrounds. These celebrations showcase the rich tapestry of Islamic traditions and provide an opportunity for Muslims to express their religious identity while also promoting understanding and interfaith dialogue.

Eid al-Fitr is a cherished holiday that brings Muslims together in gratitude, joy, and unity. Through fasting, prayer, acts of charity, and celebrations, Muslims in the United States and around the world commemorate the end of Ramadan and embrace the values of compassion, gratitude, and community. Eid al-Fitr serves as a reminder of the importance of faith, self-reflection, and the shared humanity that connects us all.

Chinese New Year - Embracing Tradition and Renewal

(falls between late January and mid-February)

Chinese New Year, also known as Lunar New Year or Spring Festival, is one of the most significant and widely celebrated holidays in Chinese culture. In this chapter, we delve into the history, customs, and vibrant festivities of Chinese New Year as observed in the United States. From the colorful parades to the symbolic rituals and mouth watering feasts, Chinese New Year offers a captivating glimpse into the rich heritage and traditions of the Chinese community.

Origins and Significance:
The roots of Chinese New Year can be traced back thousands of years to ancient Chinese mythology and folklore. Legend has it that the festival originated as a means to ward off a mythical beast called Nian, who would appear on the eve of the new year to terrorize villages. To protect themselves, the people discovered that Nian was afraid of loud noises, bright colors, and fire, leading to the practice of setting off fireworks, wearing red clothing, and hanging red lanterns during the festivities.

Preparations and Spring Cleaning:
In the weeks leading up to Chinese New Year, families embark on a flurry of preparations to ensure a fresh start to the coming year. The tradition of thorough spring cleaning is observed, symbolizing the removal of any negative energy or bad luck from the home. Every nook and cranny is meticulously scrubbed, and homes are adorned with auspicious decorations such as paper cutouts, couplets, and images of the Chinese zodiac animal associated with the upcoming year.

Reunion and Family Celebrations:

Central to Chinese New Year is the concept of family reunion, where loved ones come together to honor their ancestors and enjoy shared festivities. For many Chinese-Americans, Chinese New Year is a time to reconnect with relatives and strengthen familial bonds. Elaborate feasts are prepared, featuring traditional dishes that hold symbolic meanings, such as whole fish for abundance and dumplings for prosperity. The reunion dinner, known as the "biggest feast of the year," is a highly anticipated event filled with laughter, stories, and cherished traditions.

Lion and Dragon Dances:
The pulsating beats of drums and cymbals fill the streets as colorful lion and dragon dancers make their way through the community. Lion and dragon dances are iconic performances during Chinese New Year, believed to bring good luck and ward off evil spirits. The dynamic movements, acrobatics, and synchronized formations of the dancers captivate spectators of all ages. The lion's energetic leaps and playful interactions with the crowd, and the sinuous undulations of the dragon, create an electrifying atmosphere of joy and excitement.

Fireworks and Firecrackers:
As the sun sets on New Year's Eve, the night sky comes alive with dazzling displays of fireworks and firecrackers. The explosions and vivid bursts of colors are believed to drive away evil spirits and ensure a prosperous year ahead. Chinese communities in the United States organize grand fireworks shows, attracting locals and visitors alike. The sight and sound of fireworks illuminate the darkness, filling hearts with anticipation and wonder.

Red Envelopes and the Lion's Nian Gao:
One of the most beloved traditions of Chinese New Year is the exchange of red envelopes, known as hongbao. These red envelopes contain monetary gifts and are given to children, unmarried relatives, and employees as a symbol of good luck and blessings for the year ahead. Another delightful custom is the Lion's Nian Gao, a special sweet rice cake made in the shape of a lion's head. The Nian Gao is shared among family members and friends, representing wishes for a sweet and prosperous year.

Parades and Cultural Festivities:
Across the United States, vibrant parades and cultural festivals take place during Chinese New Year. Major cities such as San Francisco, New York, and Los Angeles host elaborate processions featuring ornate floats, traditional costumes, lion and dragon dances, and martial arts performances. These parades showcase the diversity and vibrancy of the Chinese community, while also welcoming people from various backgrounds to partake in the festivities. Cultural exhibitions, live performances, and art

displays provide opportunities for everyone to appreciate the richness of Chinese culture.

Wrapping Up the Celebrations:
The culmination of Chinese New Year festivities comes with the Lantern Festival, held on the fifteenth day of the lunar calendar. This magical event illuminates the night sky with a sea of glowing lanterns, each crafted with care and adorned with intricate designs. Families gather to release lanterns into the air, symbolizing hopes, dreams, and aspirations for the year ahead. Lantern riddles, performances, and delectable treats add to the enchanting atmosphere of the Lantern Festival.

Chinese New Year in the United States is a testament to the enduring traditions and cultural heritage of the Chinese community. It is a time of joy, reunion, and renewal, as families and friends come together to honor their roots and embrace the future. Through the vibrant parades, sumptuous feasts, and age-old customs, Chinese New Year serves as a bridge between generations, preserving cherished traditions while forging new connections in a multicultural society. The spirit of unity, gratitude, and celebration that permeates this festive occasion brings communities together and leaves a lasting imprint of cultural richness and diversity.

Cinco de Mayo - Celebrating Mexican Heritage and Unity

(May 5th)

Cinco de Mayo, meaning "Fifth of May" in Spanish, is a vibrant and widely celebrated holiday in the United States that commemorates the Mexican army's victory over the French forces at the Battle of Puebla on May 5, 1862. In this chapter, we explore the history, significance, and festive traditions of Cinco de Mayo as observed across the nation. From colorful parades to lively music and dance, Cinco de Mayo is a time to embrace Mexican heritage, culture, and unity.

The Battle of Puebla and its Historical Context:
To understand the significance of Cinco de Mayo, we delve into the historical context of the Battle of Puebla. In the mid-19th century, Mexico faced political instability and financial difficulties. During this time, France, led by Emperor Napoleon III, sought to establish a French presence in Mexico. The Mexican army, despite being outnumbered and ill-equipped, bravely defended their country and achieved a remarkable victory over the French forces in the city of Puebla. Although the French later occupied Mexico City, the Battle of Puebla became a symbol of Mexican resilience and patriotism.

Celebrations in the United States:
Cinco de Mayo celebrations in the United States have evolved over time, transforming into vibrant displays of Mexican culture, heritage, and unity. From small community gatherings to large-scale festivals, people of all backgrounds come together to celebrate this festive occasion. Cities with significant Mexican-American populations, such as Los Angeles, Chicago, and San Antonio, host elaborate parades, cultural exhibitions, and musical performances that showcase the richness and diversity of Mexican traditions.

Traditional Music and Dance:

Music and dance play a central role in Cinco de Mayo celebrations. From the lively rhythms of mariachi bands to the exuberant movements of traditional folk dances, the sounds and sights of Mexican music and dance captivate audiences and create an atmosphere of joy and celebration. Mariachi bands, with their iconic sombreros and charro suits, serenade the crowds with their heartfelt melodies, while folk dance troupes showcase the vibrant costumes and intricate footwork that embody Mexico's diverse regional traditions.

Delicious Cuisine and Culinary Delights:
No Cinco de Mayo celebration is complete without indulging in the tantalizing flavors of Mexican cuisine. From savory tacos and tamales to spicy salsas and refreshing margaritas, the culinary offerings of Cinco de Mayo tantalize the taste buds and showcase the diverse and flavorful aspects of Mexican gastronomy. Street vendors, food trucks, and restaurants serve up traditional dishes with authentic ingredients, allowing revelers to savor the true essence of Mexican cuisine.

Arts, Crafts, and Visual Delights:
Cinco de Mayo festivities also provide a platform for Mexican artists and artisans to showcase their talents. Art exhibitions featuring traditional and contemporary Mexican artwork, craft markets offering handmade jewelry and textiles, and visual displays of Mexican history and culture provide a glimpse into the rich artistic heritage of Mexico. Intricate papel picado, vibrant murals, and intricate pottery are just a few examples of the visual delights that adorn Cinco de Mayo celebrations.

Educational and Cultural Programs:
In recent years, efforts to educate the public about the historical significance of Cinco de Mayo have gained momentum. Schools, museums, and cultural centers organize educational programs, lectures, and exhibits to foster understanding and appreciation for Mexican history and culture. These initiatives aim to go beyond the surface-level festivities and provide a deeper understanding of the struggles and triumphs that Cinco de Mayo represents.

Community Unity and Pride:
Cinco de Mayo serves as a catalyst for community unity and pride, bridging cultural divides and fostering a sense of belonging among Mexican-Americans and the wider community. The holiday brings together people of all backgrounds, encouraging dialogue, cultural exchange, and mutual respect. It is a time to honor and celebrate the contributions of Mexican-Americans to the fabric of American society, highlighting the value of diversity and inclusion.

Cinco de Mayo is a cherished holiday that unites communities in celebration of Mexican heritage, culture, and unity. Through vibrant parades, lively music and dance, delicious cuisine, and educational programs, Cinco de Mayo provides a platform to honor the bravery of the Mexican army at the Battle of Puebla while celebrating the rich tapestry of Mexican culture. This festive occasion encourages cultural exchange, fosters community unity, and serves as a reminder of the enduring ties between Mexico and the United States. Whether you join a local parade, indulge in Mexican cuisine, or learn about Mexican history and traditions, Cinco de Mayo offers a vibrant and joyous experience that leaves a lasting impression of unity, pride, and cultural appreciation.

Oktoberfest - A Bavarian Celebration in the United States

(typically takes place in September or October)

Oktoberfest, the iconic Bavarian festival, has transcended its origins in Munich, Germany, and become a beloved cultural celebration across the United States. In this chapter, we embark on a journey through the history, traditions, and festivities of Oktoberfest as it unfolds in American cities and communities. From the lively beer tents to the vibrant parades and traditional music, Oktoberfest in the United States offers an authentic taste of Bavarian culture and an opportunity for people of all backgrounds to come together in joyous celebration.

Origins and Evolution of Oktoberfest:
We delve into the origins of Oktoberfest, tracing its roots back to the wedding of Bavarian Crown Prince Ludwig and Princess Therese in 1810. The grand festivities held in Munich to commemorate their nuptials set the stage for what would become an annual tradition. Over the years, Oktoberfest grew in popularity, transforming from a local celebration into an internationally recognized event. We explore the cultural significance of Oktoberfest in Bavaria and how it has been adapted and embraced by communities across the United States.

Oktoberfest in the United States:
American cities and towns have embraced the spirit of Oktoberfest, hosting their own versions of the festival that pay homage to Bavarian traditions. From large-scale events in cities like Cincinnati, Ohio, and Milwaukee, Wisconsin, to smaller gatherings in German-American communities, Oktoberfest in the United States captures the essence of the original celebration. We delve into the unique characteristics and regional

variations of Oktoberfest festivities, showcasing the diverse ways in which this cherished tradition is celebrated.

Beer Tents and Brews:
At the heart of Oktoberfest in the United States are the iconic beer tents, where revelers gather to raise their steins and toast to the spirit of the festival. We explore the rich brewing heritage and the wide variety of German-style beers that are showcased during Oktoberfest. From the traditional Märzen lagers to wheat beers and specialty brews, Oktoberfest offers a unique opportunity to savor the flavors of Bavarian beer culture. We also highlight the role of local breweries and craft beer establishments in elevating the Oktoberfest experience for beer enthusiasts.

Authentic Bavarian Cuisine:
Oktoberfest is not just about beer; it is also a celebration of Bavarian cuisine. We delve into the mouthwatering delights that grace the tables at Oktoberfest celebrations in the United States. From hearty sausages and pretzels to savory schnitzels and comforting sauerkraut, Bavarian cuisine takes center stage, satisfying appetites and transporting taste buds to the heart of Germany. We explore the traditional dishes and culinary traditions associated with Oktoberfest, highlighting the skill and craftsmanship that goes into creating these flavorful delights.

Music, Dance, and Entertainment:
No Oktoberfest celebration is complete without lively music, festive dances, and entertaining performances. We delve into the vibrant sounds of traditional oompah bands, whose energetic melodies fill the air and set the tone for merriment and revelry. We also explore the captivating performances of folk dancers, showcasing the colorful costumes, intricate footwork, and cultural expressions that bring Bavarian traditions to life. From polkas to waltzes, the music and dance of Oktoberfest create an atmosphere of pure joy and celebration.

Parades and Processions:
Oktoberfest parades and processions are a visual spectacle that captivates attendees of all ages. We take a front-row seat to witness the elaborate floats, marching bands, and traditional costumes that adorn these processions. Colorful banners, horse-drawn carriages, and community groups proudly display their Bavarian heritage, creating a sense of unity and pride. Oktoberfest parades not only entertain but also serve as a vibrant expression of cultural identity and community spirit.

Preserving Tradition and Embracing Innovation:

As Oktoberfest continues to evolve in the United States, we explore the delicate balance between preserving tradition and embracing innovation. While the core elements of the festival remain steadfast, organizers and communities find creative ways to infuse modern elements and engage a broader audience. We examine the efforts to incorporate sustainable practices, showcase local artisans and performers, and offer family-friendly activities, ensuring that Oktoberfest remains a relevant and inclusive celebration for generations to come.

Oktoberfest in the United States is a celebration that bridges cultures, connects communities, and invites people of all backgrounds to experience the vibrant spirit of Bavaria. Through the beer tents, the traditional cuisine, the lively music and dance, and the sense of camaraderie that permeates the festivities, Oktoberfest offers an immersive and joyful experience. Whether you raise a stein, indulge in a bratwurst, dance to the oompah band's infectious rhythm, or simply soak in the vibrant atmosphere, Oktoberfest in the United States leaves an indelible impression of cultural exchange, unity, and the enduring spirit of celebration. Prost!

Conclusion

In the pages of this book, we have embarked on a captivating journey through the rich tapestry of holidays celebrated in the United States. From the iconic traditions of New Year's Day to the vibrant festivities of Christmas Day, we have explored the diverse cultural, historical, and social significance of each holiday. As we conclude this enlightening exploration, we reflect on the threads that bind these holidays together, weaving a tapestry of unity, tradition, and celebration.

Throughout the chapters, we have discovered that holidays in the United States are more than mere days on the calendar. They are vibrant expressions of cultural identity, opportunities for communal gathering, and reflections of our shared history. Each holiday carries its own unique story, shaped by the events, traditions, and values that have shaped the nation.

New Year's Day marks the beginning of a new chapter, filled with hope, resolutions, and aspirations for personal growth. Martin Luther King Jr. Day calls us to honor the legacy of a visionary leader who fought for justice and equality. Presidents' Day invites us to reflect on the remarkable individuals who have shaped the nation's history and guided its destiny.

Memorial Day reminds us of the sacrifices made by brave men and women who laid down their lives in service to their country. Independence Day ignites a patriotic fervor as we celebrate the birth of a nation and the principles of freedom, liberty, and democracy. Labor Day honors the contributions of hardworking Americans who have built the foundations of our society.

Columbus Day, though controversial, invites us to examine the complex historical narratives and recognize the interconnectedness of cultures. Indigenous Peoples Day offers an opportunity to honor the diverse indigenous communities that have shaped this land long before the arrival of European explorers.

Veterans Day serves as a poignant reminder of the selfless dedication and unwavering commitment of those who have served in the armed forces. Thanksgiving Day invites us to pause and express gratitude for the blessings in our lives while fostering a spirit of generosity and compassion.

Christmas Day embodies both religious and cultural significance, bringing joy, love, and togetherness as we celebrate the birth of Jesus Christ and embrace the spirit of giving.

The inclusion of holidays such as St. Patrick's Day, Diwali, Hanukkah, Eid al-Fitr, Chinese New Year, Mardi Gras, Cinco de Mayo, and Oktoberfest emphasizes the vibrant tapestry of cultures that enrich the American landscape. These celebrations showcase the diversity of traditions, customs, and cuisines that have found a home in the United States, fostering cultural exchange, understanding, and unity.

As we conclude this exploration of American holidays, we recognize that they are not stagnant entities frozen in time. Instead, they evolve, adapt, and transform, influenced by the changing dynamics of society, shifting demographics, and the ever-evolving tapestry of American identity. Holidays serve as a reminder that our traditions are not fixed, but living and breathing expressions of who we are as a nation.

In each holiday, we find moments of reflection, celebration, and unity. We witness the power of shared experiences, the bonds of community, and the enduring connections that transcend differences. Holidays remind us of our collective heritage, inspire us to embrace diversity, and foster a sense of belonging.

As the final page turns, we are left with a deeper appreciation for the cultural mosaic that is the United States, a tapestry woven together by the threads of countless celebrations. Whether we partake in the revelry, honor the solemnity, or simply bear witness to the festivities, we are part of a larger narrative that celebrates our shared humanity.